DAILY RE

To Thrive

Anita McInnis

Published by

DAYELight
PUBLISHERS

ISBN: 978-1-953759-85-6 (paperback)

This book is dedicated to some very special persons: my husband and two sons, my former co-workers from New York Presbyterian Queens, especially Donna Dann, Alex's mom, who always wants to know when the next book will be coming out, and Nurse Claudine Malcolm, who encouraged me to write the devotional.

Thank you all for believing in me, encouraging me, and challenging me. Thank you for your support. I pray you will be inspired as you read another one of my books.

Preface

My name is Anita McInnis, and I am so excited to be doing these devotionals. My prayer is that as you read, God will give you wisdom, knowledge, and understanding. Please set aside a convenient time each day to read the devotionals. May each day equip you with Godly wisdom and lead you to depend totally on God. Ask God to help you that as you read, your mind and eyes will be opened to understanding clearly what He has for you.

We cannot survive effectively if we do not have a daily spiritual bath from God and His Word. Your spirit, soul and body need it. Are you desperate for God? Can you hear His voice speaking to you? Tell Him to fill your cup as you lift it up to Him. Ephesians 3:20 states, "Now unto him that is able to do exceeding, abundantly, above all that we ask or think, according to the power that worketh in us." (KJV). Philippians 4:13 says, "I can do all things through Christ that strengthens me." (KJV).

Table of Contents

Day 1

Seeking Intimacy with God

Psalm 63:1, "O God you are my God, earnestly I seek you, my soul thirst for you, my body long for you in a dry and weary land where there is no water." (NIV).

How desperate are you for God?

I am so desperate for more of God. I want peace, more confidence, and the ability to overcome the obstacles of life. Our God is Sovereign. He is in charge, He sees, hears and knows everything. Be submissive to him; it's your responsibility. The Bible says, "Blessed are those who hunger and thirst for righteousness for they will be filled." (Matthew 6:6 – NIV).

Consistency brings stability. God did not have to create the Universe, He chose to create it. Why? God is love, and love is best expressed towards something or someone else. God created the world and people as an expression of His love. We should avoid reducing God's creation to mere scientific terms. Remember that God created the universe because He loves each of us.

What do we know about God and ourselves?

About God:

- Our God is creative.
- As the Creator, He is distinct from the creation.
- He is eternal and in control of the world.

About Ourselves:
- Since God chose to create us, we are valuable in His eyes.
- We are more important than the animals.
- We are given a responsibility for the environment and the other creatures that share our planet.
- God is pleased with how He made us. If at times you feel worthless or of little value, remember, God made you for a good reason; you are valuable to Him.

Adam had a perfect relationship in a perfect environment, in the cool of the day, special time, special environment (see Genesis 3:8). This is where God can get your undivided attention. Man was created for fellowship and not worship; there was no need for worship in the garden.

The effect of sin is separation. Here are four things Eve did:

- She looked

Temptation begins with seeing something you want. 2 Timothy 2:22 states that you should "Flee the evil desires of youth, and pursue righteousness." (NIV).

Do you have a recurring temptation that is difficult to resist?

_____

_____

_____

Running away is sometimes considered a cowardly act, but wise people realize that removing themselves physically from temptation can be the most courageous action to take.

- She took
- She ate
- She gave

These are still temptations that affect us today, but 1 John 2:16 tells us, "For everything in the world—the cravings of sinful man, the lust of his eyes and the boasting of what he has and does comes not from the Father but from the world." (NIV).

God wants to meet with man.

If you are lonely or thirsty for something in your life, remember David's prayer in Psalm 63:1-8. Only God alone can satisfy our deepest longings.

Think of a time when you felt really lonely. What did you do about it?

_____

_____

_____

Day 2

Prayer Produces Intimacy

Christianity is a relationship with Jesus Christ. John 3:16 states, "For God so loved the world…" (KJV). God desires to have a relationship with us. It is very important to God; therefore, it should be important to us also. As we commit ourselves to grow in intimacy with God through prayer, it is important that we examine biblical accounts of people who had an intimate walk with God. David, in spite of his sins and issues, had a longing for God; "O God, you are my God. Earnestly I seek you: my soul thirsts for you, my body longs for you in a dry and weary land where there is no water." (Psalm 63:1 – NIV).

Our greatest adventure in life is seeking God; our greatest discovery is finding God, and our greatest fulfillment is doing the will of God, How can we grow in this area of intimacy and develop such a passion for God?

- Read your Bible daily.
- Spend time in prayer.
- Spend time with people who have a passion for God.
- Fast and pray.

The devil wants to steal our joy and create chaos in our lives. We have to counter his crafty schemes by doing all of the above. The Word of God is our defense against the devil.

In the Old Testament, people approached God through priests. After Jesus' resurrection, believers approach God directly. We approach God not because of our own merit but because Jesus, our great High Priest, has made us acceptable unto God:

1. To whom you pray.
2. For whom you pray.

Prayer is a relationship with God. It is the greatest time-saver; it saves a lot of time and heartaches. Pray before you plan and as you plan, pray. Cultivate and develop a relationship with God. 1 John 2:5-6 states, "But if anyone obeys his word, God's love is truly made complete in Him. This is how we know we are in him. Whoever claims to live in him must walk as Jesus did." (NIV).

How do we maintain this relationship? We must obey His teaching and follow His example of complete obedience to God and loving service to people. This will enhance our fellowship with God, our Father. Fellowship is taken from the Greek word KOINONIA which means "common." It is translated as "communion" and means to "join participation."

"God, who has called you into fellowship with His son Jesus Christ our Lord, is faithful. I appeal to you brothers, in the name of Jesus Christ, that all of you agree with one another so that there be no division among you and that you may be perfectly united in mind and thoughts." (1 Corinthians 1:9-10 - NIV).

To pray means to communicate with God. The key to effective prayer is understanding God's purpose for your life. Prayer is not an option for believers; it is a necessity to fulfill God's purpose in the world and our individual lives.

When I started dating my husband, he told me one of the most important things he wanted in the relationship was communication. I always want to spend as much time with him as possible, as much I want him to do the same with me. We always have conversations about so many things. Just to be together is so great: driving together, laughing, and getting a better understanding of each other. God wants us to feel this way and even greater about Him.

If you want a deep relationship with God, prayer is the key that will awaken and strengthen your desire for Him. Worship Him; you can find worship music and sing along. Read the Bible daily and always have paper and pen at your bedside, especially when you go to bed at night, because you never know what He may want to tell you. Listen attentively. Many of us are good at talking and do not listen when we should. I was taught that you should use ninety percent (90%) for listening and the remaining ten percent (10%) for talking.

Today, God's desire is that you have a relationship with Him. Philippians 3:10 states, "I want to know Christ and the power of His resurrection and the fellowship of sharing in his suffering becoming like him in His death." (NIV). Focus on God just the same as when you are going into surgery and leave your life in the doctors' hand. Pretend that you are in surgery and God is going to operate. It will hurt, but in the fullness of time, you will be healed.

If we do not pray, heaven cannot intervene in earths' affairs. How do you know when a relationship needs to end? Are they adding value or taking away their benefits? Some of the problems we are now facing are as a result of the people we embrace. Jesus made regular deposits in prayer so He could make regular withdrawals of power when He needed it. Sometimes Jesus prayed all through the night, and other times He was up praying before dawn. It was the secret to His effectiveness in ministry. We need to stay prayed up! It is the secret to a victorious Christian life.

List at least three ways you are going to have an intimate relationship with God.

1. _____

2. _____

3. _____

Day 3

Who Are You Impressing?

" Am I now trying to win the approval of men, or of God? Or am I trying to please men? If I were still trying to please men, I would not be a servant of Christ." (Galatians 1:10 - NIV).

Do you spend your life trying to please everybody? Whose approval are you seeking—others or God's? Pray for the courage to seek God's approval above anyone else's.

The best impression is when you are being yourself and showing genuine interest to know others.

We may impress people with our strengths, but we often connect best with them through our struggles. If you want to motivate someone, avoid telling them about all you have accomplished. Instead, talk about the tests or trials you went through to get where you are today. They will think: if God can do it for him or her, He will do it for me. You will give them hope.

Keep pushing; there has to be pushing; never give up hope, all things are working for your good. One day you will look back on everything you have been through and thank God for it. Do not give in or give up. Sometimes we are engulfed by sorrows and despair, and we cry, "Where is God?" Daniel and thousands of men from his country had been deported to a foreign land after Judah was conquered by idolaters. Instead of giving in or giving up, this courageous young man held fast to his faith in God. It was an active faith, obeying God with courage and doing what was right.

David knew that despite the circumstances, God was sovereign and was working out His plan for us. God is sovereign. In the book of Daniel, you can watch God work and find your security in His sovereignty. There is something about going through the fire that will change your attitude. Your spirit is humbled when you go through the fire. I have learned some lessons while going through the fire. God says, if we suffer with Him, we will also reign with Him; if we deny Him, He also will deny us (see 2 Timothy 2:12). Hold on, my child, joy comes in the morning.

Are you a man-pleaser in any way? How so?

_____

_____

_____

_____

_____

_____

Day 4

There Is A Cause

"And David said, what have I now done? Is there not a cause." (1 Samuel 17:29 – KJV).

Criticism could not stop David while the rest of the army stood around. He knew the importance of taking action, and with God fighting for him, there was no reason to wait. People may try to discourage you with negative comments or mockery, but continue to do what you know is right. By doing what is right, you will be pleasing God, whose opinion matters most.

Sometimes our plans, even the ones we think God has approved, must be placed on hold indefinitely. Like David, we can use this waiting time profitably. We can choose to learn and grow in our present circumstances, whatever they may be. David's problem was not so much the giant but his brothers. Many times it is not the "stuff" but the people.

David went on a mission with food for his brothers, but he heard something else when he went there. He did not care what Eliab, his oldest brother, thought about him; he knew there was a cause. He knew he would not be alone when he faced Goliath.

18

He looked at his situation from God's point of view. Once we are seeing clearly, we can fight more effectively. People may try to discourage us with negative comments or mockery, but continue to do what you know is right. By doing what is right, you will be pleasing God.

David rose up early; you have to catch things in the early stage. Many of us pray early in the mornings. You do not come to a certain place in your life by accident; there is a cause. God often uses simple and ordinary objects to accomplish His task in the world. It is most important that they be dedicated to Him for His use. What do you have that God can use? Anything and everything is a possible instrument for Him. Moses used a staff to work miracles before Pharoah. David used a small stone to kill Goliath, and Jesus used five loaves and two fish to feed a crowd of over five thousand people. What will you use in your circumstances?

List two things you have that God can use.

1. _____

2. _____

Day 5

Shift Your Mindset To One Of Positivity

Why are you cutting yourself?

"Night and day among the tombs and in the hills he would cry out and cut himself with stones." (Mark 5:5 – NIV).

This man lived in the tombs and no one could bind him, not even with a chain. No one was able to subdue him. Can you imagine? He had an unclean spirit; to him, his life had no value because he was cutting his own flesh with stones. Today, many men, women, and even our young people are cutting themselves. I have seen young people who become suicidal because of pressure, anxiety, fear, among other things. They cut themselves; some do the cutting physically, while others do it mentally. They may act as if all is well, but when they are alone, they cut themselves and bleed.

Many suffer from insecurity; they do not love themselves. 1 John 4:20 states "Whoever claims to love God yet hates a brother or sister is a liar. For whoever does not love their brother and sister, whom they have seen, cannot love God, whom they have not seen." (NIV). Your self-image is very important. Who are you? It does not matter what others think about you, it matters what you think about yourself and how God sees you. You will develop self-hatred when you start cutting yourself. Stop saying things like, "I am getting older," "My age is off the calendar," "I cannot find anyone," "I am not good at my job," "No one loves me," or "I am depressed, fearful of living by myself" and the list goes on. STOP IT NOW! Come from this downward spiral because this is not what God wants for you. "For I know the plans I have for you," declares the Lord, "plans to prosper you and not to harm you, plans to give you hope and a future." (Jeremiah 29:11 – NIV). Change your perspective on life. Life is short but we know who holds tomorrow, and we know who holds our hands.

The man with the unclean spirit was cutting himself and doing far more damage than any other person had ever been able to do to him. The same holds true for us. We do far more damage to ourselves than others do.

I know me and I love me. I do have faults, but I love me. Be who you are; created in God's image. Start believing in you, that God made you, He loves you, and that is all the reason you need for loving yourself. Stop cutting yourself. Shift your mentality to one of self-confidence and belief; please do not create a cycle of negativity.

Name some things you are hard on yourself about that you want to stop now.

1. _____

2. _____

3. _____

Day 6

Sudden Awakening In Our Lives

Luke 15:17, "When he came to his senses, he said, 'How many of my father's hired servants have food to spare, and here I am starving to death!'" (NIV).

The whole story is about the prodigal son. This young man got a sudden awakening that took place when God finally got his attention. When he came to his senses, he sat straight up and suddenly realized what his life had become. He did not hear the alarm until he got to the pig pen. He made his request from his dad: "I want my portion now! I am not waiting." The famine came on the land, and he lost everything. He was working with pigs.

According to the Mosaic law, pigs were unclean animals. Jews would not even touch pigs. Looking at a Jew feeding pigs was a great humiliation, and the food that the pigs had touched was to be degraded beyond belief. This young man, like many who are rebellious and immature, wanted to be free and live as he pleased, and he had to hit rock bottom before he came to his senses. How did he not see the warning signs? How about you?

You do not have to hit rock bottom before you come to your senses.

It is sad that it often takes great sorrow and tragedy to cause people to look to the only One who can help them. Are you trying to live life your own way by selfishly pushing aside any responsibility or commitment that gets in your way? Stop before you hit rock bottom. You will save yourself and your family much grief.

Sudden awakenings you did not see coming can include:

- He filed for a divorce.
- Becoming an alcoholic.
- The pregnancy test is positive; not married and singing on the choir.
- Got fired for embezzlement.

Your own actions and choices will bring about consequences. Jesus said "Then you will know the truth, and the truth will set you free." (John 8:32 - NIV). Have you ever had a moment where you are trying to live from your own strength rather than out of the power of God? You then realize that you are stressed about money because you are putting your trust in money more than God.

Whatever is your sudden awakening, do something about it instead of wrestling with guilt and shame. As for the prodigal son, for him to come to that realization, he had to have some time alone, some time to think. At times when God speaks, He does in solitude and silence. I want God to speak to me; say something to me, God. There is a song that says, "Open the eyes of my heart, Lord. I want to see You!." That is my prayer.

Elijah went to the mountain to meet with God. While he waited, there was a strong wind blowing, and he thought God must be in the wind, but He wasn't. The wind died down, then the earthquake but God was not there. There was a fire, but He was not in the fire either. These are ways we would expect God to speak, but He often speaks in a gentle whisper (see 1 Kings 19:12). That was when Elijah heard God.

How will you hear from Him today?

My sudden awakening was:

_____

_____

_____

_____

_____

_____

_____

_____

_____

_____

_____

_____

_____

Day 7

How Honest Are You To Yourself?

It is time to go back.

Luke 15:18 says, "I will set out and go back to my father and say to him: Father, I have sinned against heaven and against you." (NIV).

He was very honest with himself.

How many times do you talk to yourself? Have you ever learned something about yourself or had someone tell you something and it completely changed things and you were awakened to some truth? What did you do then? Many of us are awakened, but we struggle with honesty. We cannot say, "I was wrong" and "I am sorry."

There was no one else with the prodigal son but the pigs. Sometimes the hardest conversation to have is with yourself. Honesty begins when we look in the mirror and speak the truth about what we see. Tell the truth about yourself to yourself. The prodigal son "said to himself" (see Luke 15:17-19). He was honest with himself about what he deserved. That kind of honesty is difficult. The person who is looking in the mirror (you) is the hardest person to be honest with.

Immediate action is where most of us get stuck, but it is important to recognize that without the action, the story will never change. Look what happened to the young man; he came to his senses and got up. Luke 15:20 says, "So he got up and went to his father." (NIV). If he did not come to his senses in verse 17, then verse 20 would not be. He would still be with the pigs, living in brokenness.

What action do you need to take? When are you going to get up? Can you call out for "Help?" God's love is constant, patient, and welcoming. He will search for us and give us opportunities to respond, but He will not force us to come to Him. Like the father in this story, God waits patiently for us to come to our senses.

Here are some key ways to be honest with yourself:

- Do some reflection.
- Admit you made a mistake, and you are wrong.
- Trust your intuition.
- Avoid overthinking.
- Have someone you can trust. Know when to trust your gut.

Are you willing to give God what He wants from you today?

- Yes
- No
- Still not there yet

Day 8

Time For A Checkup

1 Corinthians 11:28 says, "But let a man examine himself, and so let him eat of that bread, and drink of that cup." (KJV). Paul wrote this to the Corinthians, some of whom were eating in an unworthy manner. Paul says everyone should examine himself, and after your examination, then you can participate in the Lord's supper. People were just rushing in and taking communion without knowing the significance, so Paul had to address them. Those who took it unworthily were guilty of sinning against the body and blood of the Lord. Instead of honoring His sacrifice, they were sharing in the guilt of those who crucified Christ. In reality, none of us are worth it; we are all sinners saved by grace. Therefore, we should prepare ourselves for communion through confession of our sins and resolution of differences with others. As Christians, we should endeavor to be Christ-like. The essential disciplines of prayer, Bible study, and worship equip us to run with vigor and stamina. Don't merely observe from the grandstand; don't just turn out to jog a couple of laps each morning. Train diligently; your spiritual progress depends on it.

Is it time for your checkup? Every year I have a physical, and many people do. It is that periodic visit to the doctor's office where we are poked with needles, screened, and studied. It is something that can be easy to dread and even fear. I personally do not like mammograms, but I have to do it. A Pap smear is even worst, but I must do it because I want my examination to be done so I know what is going on in my body, trusting God that all is well. Amidst all the discomfort, I do it, and then I can hardly wait to get the results and to hear what the doctor will tell me. The same is true spiritually in the life of the Christian believer. We need to pause from time to time and reflect on the condition of our hearts and lives. Today, unforgiveness is a big hindrance in many people's lives. Many people are walking with healed feelings or hurt feelings.

Which are you?

Healed Feelings	OR	Hurt Feelings
Free		I am still burdened
Forgiving		Unforgiving
Accepting		Judgmental
Healed		Cold-Hearted
Refreshed		Angry/Bitter

Based on the Bible, forgiveness should characterize our lives. Forgiveness is one of the hardest things for many people. Many people say they have been hurt so badly and deeply that the mere idea of offering forgiveness to those who hurt them seems impossible. Forgiveness, in these cases, seems like we are letting people get off the hook for their transgressions. Listen, if you are really ready to do your checkup, then do it. The doctor is about to give you the results. Yes, the sharp pain in your heart is that thing that creates a barrier that prevents you from moving beyond the pain. The brokenness and pain seem unending, but God is a present help in the time of trouble, and He is waiting to help you. Are you at a crossroads as it relates to what to really do? In the face of so much brokenness in our lives and in the world, how should we respond? Should we deny it? Ignore it? Get even, which many people do? Give up? Look in the Bible for the answer—forgive.

Forgiveness will never be easy; however, only through forgiveness can healing begin. Your spiritual maturity depends on your willingness to face, forgive and forget past offenses.

Self-examination is one test no Christian is excused from. A lack of unity is one of the many challenges the church is facing today. Psalm 133:1 says, "Behold, how good and how pleasant it is for brethren to dwell together in unity." (KJV). We need the Holy Spirit to do the work in our lives. It is good to be passionate about the things of God, but Jesus tells us it is more valuable to love, and love does not dishonor people, especially those we disagree with.

Day 9

What Difference Do You Make?

Mark 2:1-2 says, "A few days later, when Jesus again entered Capernaum, the people heard that he had come home. They gathered in such large numbers that there was no room left, not even outside the door, and he preached the word to them." (NIV).

Jesus turned this city upside down when He went there.

How does someone view you as a Christian? What can people say about you, even at home? Do you make a difference among your unsaved family? Can they really say you are a child of God? Whatever you participate in, whichever group you are in, your presence ought to be felt. When you are on your job and you walk into the lunchroom, office or whatever the department you work in, your coworkers, the clients, customers, suppliers, vendors, everyone you associate yourself with ought to be blessed because you are God's servant and you make a difference. Your presence should provoke change. Wherever God is present, change happens; people's attitude change and situations are turned around.

Paul said, "I pressed towards the mark of the high calling." I am not perfect but I am pressing. Each day I get up in the morning I am pressing. Energy is measured by motion. I cannot do much sitting down. The devil would want me to sit down and stay down, but I have a determination. I endeavor to reach my destination.

"But he knoweth the way that I take: when he hath tried me, I shall come forth as gold." (Job 23:10 - KJV).

"The steps of a good man are ordered by the Lord: and he delighteth in his way." (Psalm 37:23 – KJV).

I am far from perfect, but I endeavor to live a life of integrity. I was once at a job and my manager did not want to see a difficult customer, so she told me to tell the customer she was not there. I told her I was sorry, but I could not. As Christians, our light should always shine. You are the salt of the earth (see Matthew 5:13). When we do those things, the same people we do it for will turn around and say, "She said she is a Christian and she just lied for me." Think about it. Also, if I am to meet with someone, I never say I am on my way when I am still home. I would say, "I am going through the door now and I will be on my way." We should be men and women of integrity.

In the New Testament, when a woman came to Simon's house with an alabaster jar and poured perfume on Jesus' head, those present saw it as a waste. This expensive perfume was worth a year's common wages, so some of the people present thought it could have been used to help the poor. However, Jesus commended her. He said she had done a beautiful thing to Him (see Mark 14:6). We can choose to let Christ's life shine in our lives every day and display His beauty to the world. To some, it may seem a waste, but let us have a willing heart to serve Him.

In what ways can Jesus say you have done beautiful things for Him?

1. _____

2. _____

3. _____

Day 10

Areas Where Forgiveness Might Be Very Difficult

As we go through life, the issues and challenges that I go through may not be the same as what you go through, but we all have challenges. We have different areas of brokenness in our lives, such as:

- Social—Bullying, cyberbullying, name-calling, loss of reputation from lies and gossip.
- Physical—Parental neglect of a child's physical needs, sexual or domestic abuse.
- Spiritual—Church leader's misuse of authority. Rejection from church family; individual's private sins that damage their relationship with God.
- Emotional—Divorce, infidelity, lying, abandonment by parents, betrayal by a trusted friend or confidant.

Forgiveness is possible, and God desires for us to forgive. 2 Chronicles 7:14 says, "If my people, who are called by my name, will humble themselves and pray and seek my face and turn from their wicked ways, then I will hear from heaven, and

I will forgive their sin and will heal their land." (NIV). God answers with four conditions for forgiveness:

1. Humble yourself by admitting your sins.
2. Pray to God asking for forgiveness.
3. Seek God continually.
4. Turn from sinful behavior.

True repentance is more than talk, it is changed behavior. Whether we sin individually, as a group, or as a nation, following these steps will lead to forgiveness. God will answer our earnest prayers. In these areas of difficulties, God will make it possible for you.

In the New Testament, we see God's desire to forgive being expressed most clearly in the life and death of His Son. Jesus' sinless life and voluntary death atoned for the world's sins. He bore the ultimate judgment of sin so we don't have to. God forgives us because He loves us. Therefore, my friends, I want you to know that through Jesus, the forgiveness of sin is proclaimed to you (see Acts 13:38).

But God demonstrates His own love for us in this: while we were still sinners, Christ died for us. (Romans 5:8 - NIV).

In Him we have redemption through His blood, the forgiveness of sins, in accordance with the riches of God's grace. (Ephesians 1:7 - NIV).

In what ways are you having problems forgiving?

_____

_____

_____

Day 11

The Parable Of The Unmerciful Servant

In Matthew 18:21, Peter asked Jesus a question. He asked, "Lord, how often shall my brother sin against me, and I forgive him? Up to seven times?" (NKJV). Peter must have thought that seven times was very generous. Jesus answered, "I do not say to you, up to seven times, but up to seventy times seven." (Matthew 18:22 – NKJV). I am sure that seemed impossible to Peter. Jesus then explains why we should forgive with this story about a king and a servant who owes him a lot of money.

Matthew 18:23-34 tells the story of a king who was owed a massive amount of money by his servant who was unable to pay. Because the servant was not able to pay, the master ordered the whole family to be sold to repay him. The servant begged for more time, and the King was moved with compassion. The entire debt was canceled and the servant walked away a debt-free man instead of being sold into slavery as the law allowed.

This servant then went to someone who owed him little, and instead of paying it forward, he became violent, grabbed, and choked the man, refusing to listen to his cries for mercy. He threw his fellow servant into prison.

When the unmerciful servant's actions were exposed, look what happened:

- He was reported to the King by fellow servants (see Matthew 18:31).
- There was no compassion this time as the King became angry.
- The servant was called "wicked" by the King.
- The King sent him to jail until he could pay back everything he owed (see Matthew 18:34).

The lesson we should learn from this is: it is the same way our heavenly Father will treat each of us unless we forgive our brother or sister from our heart. Our debt to God is enormous, and His forgiveness is extravagant. In light of this, Jesus allows no excuses for withholding forgiveness from others.

Are you the merciful servant or the unmerciful?

How so?

_____

_____

_____

_____

_____

_____

Day 12

Separated To Be Elevated

Genesis 12:1 says, "The Lord had said to Abram, "Go from your country, your people and your father's household to the land I will show you."" (NIV).

God promised to bless Abram and make him great, but there was one condition. Abram had to do what God wanted him to do. This meant leaving his home and friends and traveling to a new land where God promised to build a great nation from Abram's family. Abram obeyed, walking away from his home for God's promise of even greater blessings in the future. Today, God may be trying to lead you to a place of greater service and usefulness for Him. Don't let the comfort and security of your present position make you miss God's plan for you.

God's voice makes a difference, and He is about to separate you. Are you ready to be separated? God took Abram to Canaan, a land flowing with milk and honey. You must get rid of things you are attached to before God will elevate you. Separation can be lonely. Between the separation and the elevation, it can be a very lonely period. If you want to develop greatness in your life, develop a team of positive influential people who are success-driven and believe in you. I have at least ten people like that in my life.

God wants you to listen to Him and hear when He speaks. It can and will hurt at times, but you have to go through it. God will break you to make you. When the storms of life come, you will make it through. You must choose wisely the kind of influences and people in your life, the kind of books you read, movies you watch, and the materials you allow into your mind. Remember, the mind is a powerful thing.

If you want to be healthy but you cannot separate from junk food, how long do you think your dream of health will last. It is the same thing in the spiritual realm; you must separate yourself from many things. Drop some friends, draw the line, and stop going some places. God said, "Come out from among them be ye separated." There is a song that says "Zion is calling you to a higher place of praise, to stand upon the mountain and to magnify His name. To tell all the people of every nation that He reigns. Zion is calling you to a higher place of praise."

God called Abram from the godless, self-centered city of Ur to a fertile region called Canaan, where a God-centered, moral nation could be established. Though small in dimension, the land of Canaan was the focal point for most of the history of Israel as well as for the rise of Christianity. This small land given to one man, Abram, had a tremendous impact on world history. Abram built altars to God for two reasons:

1. Prayer and worship.
2. As reminders of God's promise to bless him.

Abram could not survive spiritually without regularly renewing his love and loyalty to God. Building altars helped Abram remember that God was at the center of his life. Regular worship helps us remember what God desires and motivates us to obey Him. Isaiah 43:19 says, "See, I am doing a new thing! Now it springs up; do you not perceive it? I am making a way in the wilderness and streams in the wasteland." (NIV).

The Israelites were slaves in Egypt, and every time they cried to God, He would hear and deliver them. A new Exodus took place through a new dessert. The past miracles were nothing compared to what God will do for His people in the future. God wants us to hear Him.

"I am the Lord, Your Holy one, Israel's Creator, your King." (Isaiah 43:15 – NIV).

Do not let your behavior, stubbornness, or disobedience hinder you from your elevation. Blessed people can still live in bondage.

Think about some hindrances right now that are hindering you from your elevation. Write them below:

_____

_____

_____

_____

_____

Day 13

What Do You Have In Your House (Part 1)

E lisha replied to her, "How can I help you? Tell me, what do you have in your house?" "Your servant has nothing there at all," she said, "except a small jar of olive oil." (2 Kings 4:2 – NIV).

Israel was divided into two kingdoms: the northern and southern. This story took place in the northern Kingdom that was run by a king who ignored God. The king was the son of Ahab and Jezebel, who introduced Baal worship in Israel. The nation was in turmoil, the enemies were getting stronger, the economy was getting weaker, and the leadership of the country was trusting their own wisdom more than God. In the midst of this, as a result of the national crisis, families were facing a personal crisis of their own. We all see or hear what is happening at the border between the United States and Mexico with the separation of families.

This woman was the wife of a man from the company of the prophets, and she cried out to Elisha. Who are you crying out to today? Her husband was dead, and the creditors would come and make slaves out of her sons. Maybe the husband did not do a good job with the family debt. There was no life insurance money left behind, and now the family was in trouble. What was she going to do? To make things worse, the creditors were at the door demanding payment. She probably did not get the time to mourn the loss of her husband. Maybe she was up in age and could not get employment. The creditors would settle the score—take her sons until the debt was paid. How do you feel so far about this story? What if it was you? For me, this is very disturbing. I have two sons, and the thought of someone taking them from me is very hard and disturbing to even think about.

This woman did not have the time to think and think fast. Let us reflect here a moment; let's be practical. Many of us cannot understand why we are serving God and bad things are happening to us. We may say, "It is not fair" because we are not as irresponsible as others. We have done the best we can in serving God. No one is perfect, so, for the most part, we know we are living right, yet we are experiencing the brunt of the economy, struggling financially, can't get a job, losing our homes, our children are disobedient, and struggling with our marriages. We are waiting to have those children God promised us. We still cannot find Mr. Right or Ms. Right.

This woman had a valid complaint—there was nothing left. How about your account? Do you have an overdraft on it and need divine intervention? She lost her husband and was about to lose her sons. In her old age, there was no social security for her. I imagine her sons were taking care of her, but now she was about to face loneliness, bereavement, and despair. *What else, God?*

God made a special promise for widows and orphans in the Bible. "Religion that God accepts as pure and faultless is this, to look after orphans and widows in their distress and to keep oneself from being polluted by the world." (James 1:27 - NIV). The widows were supposed to glean in the fields and vineyard to get food. They were not supposed to be oppressed or taken advantage of. Exodus 22:22-23 says, "Do not take advantage of a widow or orphan. If you do and they cry out to me, I will certainly hear their cry." (NIV). In 2 Kings 4:2 Elisha asked, "How can I help you?" (NIV). He was sensitive, concerned, and compassionate. He was willing to be involved, and so was God. Then he asked another question: "What do you have in your house?"

What do you have in your house that God can use? Your time, your heart, your availability? It is important to know the resources you have and use them to the best of your ability. God will pour out a blessing when we do.

As women, sometimes we may have too many pocketbooks in our closet and clothing we can give away, and we are keeping them. What do you have in your house?

_____

_____

_____

_____

_____

_____

_____

Day 14

What Do You Have In Your House (Part 2)

This was a very important question. This woman did not have any handouts; she was not on welfare. God would use what she had to start with. Look at the principle here; God will multiply what we surrender to Him.

Do you remember when Moses was terrified about meeting with Pharaoh? God asked him, "What is that in your hand?" (see Exodus 4:2). Moses' staff became the rod of God, a symbol of God's power.

Jesus fed 5000 plus people with a little boy's lunch that He multiplied (see John 6:1-15). Many times, God wants us to trust Him, to live by faith. God is saying, "I want you to accomplish the task. Finish what I gave you to do." Our answer, "How can I? I do not have the talent. I am not capable. I do not have the resources. I have nothing. I am poor."

There was a market for her oil. All she had to do was be obedient. Elisha responds in 2 Kings 4:3-4, "Go, borrow vessels from everywhere, from all your neighbors—empty vessels; do not gather just a few. And when you have come in, you shall shut the door behind you and your sons; then pour it into all those vessels, and set aside the full ones." (NKJV). Why couldn't the jars be multiplied as well as the oil? That sounds like a simple solution. One reason, I believe, is that it requires faith to go around to every neighbor and ask for empty jars. Everyone knew her plight. It took faith to obey Elisha. I can imagine how nervous and fearful she was. *What if it did not work?* We too are sometimes fearful. No matter how she felt, she acted with her will to obey Elisha with boldness and personal effort combined with her faith. I can only imagine her and her sons going from house to house. Maybe Elisha asked her to go to the community because they were not helping her with her debt. Every family was now involved in contributing a bottle. We have a responsibility to help the shut-ins.

In the privacy of her home, she stood with her two sons; the instruction was for her to shut the door. It was not for everyone at this point. There are times when we have to shut out some people. God will multiply what you surrender to Him. He will multiply it beyond your wildest dream. How do you think her sons felt? We need to share things with our children concerning what God is doing in our lives. We may tell our friends, but not our children.

Elisha said, "Go sell the oil!" (see 2 Kings 4:7). She had work to do; she had to take the initiative to pay her debt. We need to talk about our needs; do not get help with a closed mouth. Do not be too proud to call for help. Think about this widow and what she would have missed if she did not cry out to Elisha. What problem do you have now that you are crying out to God about? What grief have you suffered that you cannot find a reason for, that you are bitter about? are you willing to accept

46

this thing from God's hand because He gave it to you? Can you believe God will ultimately use it for your good, reveal Himself to you through it, and bring you to maturity? Will you consider it a mixed joy?

Jesus did not deserve to be falsely accused, sentenced to death, beaten, and spit upon. He willingly endured, so you and I will be forgiven of our sins and have a relationship with God that will last forever. God is an expert at taking tragedy and turning it into triumph. God is the one who is able to change and turn people's life around by giving them not only a second chance, but a fresh start. It is possible to say that in life, pain and problems come to everyone at one stage or the other in their lives. We as believers are encouraged that God is our helper and He will see us through life's challenges. God has promised that He will never leave us nor forsake us. Deuteronomy 31:6 says "Be strong and courageous. Do not be afraid or terrified because of them, for the Lord your God goes with you; he will never leave you nor forsake you." (NIV). What the devil meant for evil, God will make it good. Your pain will turn you around and drive you into your purpose—look at your journey and understand your why.

There is a seed of greatness in every one of us. Ask yourself, "What's in my hand?" We all have a passion. We all have something to get the job done. I can accept failure, but I will not accept that I will not try because we are never alone. We are powerful, and we are sitting on our seats of power.

Today, we must recognize what we have—provide vessels that are empty. We need the Holy Spirit; He is waiting to fill our emptiness. Make room for Him. Sometimes we are full of pride, unforgiveness, bitterness and the list goes on. The Holy Spirit cannot work within us when we are full of these things. The secret of a Spirit-filled life is the result of a shut door. We have to shut out some things in our lives. Only you know what you need to shut out.

What jar are you holding that you do not think is enough to make a difference? What do you need to move forward? Is it your education, money, or the right season in your life? So often we do not think we have enough to offer, or we think we do not have what it takes to succeed on God's behalf. That is not true.

What jar do you have? Is it your talent, time, or money? Are you ready to see God multiply it? Aren't you tired of holding back? Today, believe for the impossible; believe that you have faith that God will multiple what is done in His name and, remember, we are not alone. God will provide the oil if we have the jars.

Day 15

Separation For Service

As they ministered to the Lord and fasted, the Holy Spirit said, "Now separate to Me Barnabas and Saul for the work to which I have called them." Then, having fasted and prayed, and laid hands on them, they sent them away. (Acts 13:2-3 – NKJV).

Jesus chose twelve disciples and deposited in them what was needed for service. The church set apart Barnabas and Saul to the work God had for them. To set apart means to dedicate for a special purpose. We too should dedicate our pastors, missionaries, and Christian workers for their tasks. We can also dedicate ourselves to use our time, money, and talents for God's work.

Ask God what He wants you to set apart for Him. Following Paul's conversion, the Christians were understandably reluctant to welcome him. They thought his story was a trick to capture more Christians. Barnabas was the one who convinced them that their former enemy was now a vibrant believer, and his name was changed from Saul to Paul. Our tendency at times is to criticize. It may be important sometimes to point out someone's shortcomings but before we have the right to do this, we must build that person's trust through encouragement. Are you prepared to encourage those with whom you come in contact today?

Saul had a purpose in him, and God was determined to use him, even though he was a murderer. We are to be separated from all that is contrary to God's will and separated to God Himself for His use and for His glory. Barnabas and Saul were setting out on a great missionary journey and were to separate themselves to that one task, but before they separated themselves to the task, they were to be separated to the Holy Spirit. So it was separation to the Lord, and then separation to the task. 2 Corinthians 8:5 says, "And they exceeded our expectations: They gave themselves first of all to the Lord, and then by the will of God also to us." (NIV). God wants us to place ourselves utterly and absolutely at His disposal.

Can you think of anything that may be a hindrance to you stepping into your divine service for God?

Day 16

Aspiring To A Place Of Honor

There is a trustworthy saying in 1 Timothy 3:1: "Whoever aspires to be an overseer desires a noble task." (NIV).

To be a church leader (overseer) is a heavy responsibility because the church belongs to the living God. Church leaders should not be elected because they are popular, nor should they be allowed to push their way to the top. Instead, they should be chosen by the church because of their respect for the truth, both in what they believe and in how they live.

The word "honor" means a place of high regard or respect—a place of glory and dignity. When you are in a place of honor, your work carries power. People receive honor by merit. The road to honor is not for the lazy and fearful.

Factors that will bring you to a place of honor:

- Vision
  Jabez was more honorable than his brothers. His mother had named him Jabez,[a] saying, "I gave birth

to him in pain." 10 Jabez cried out to the God of Israel, "Oh, that you would bless me and enlarge my territory! Let your hand be with me, and keep me from harm so that I will be free from pain." And God granted his request. (1 Chronicles 4:9-10 - NIV).

- Prepare for what you want to do. Nothing happens without preparation. God is preparing the church for the day of honor. He is coming for a church without spot or wrinkle (see Ephesians 5:27). God prepared Moses at the house of Pharoah. He prepared David at the house of Saul.
- Jesus was prepared. He spent time being alone and preparing for His mission.

You have to know how to make sacrifices if you want to go to a place of honor. Some people want everything to be convenient. Some sleep too much. Prayer takes a lot of work. If you are not blessed, you cannot be a blessing. Not only should we seek God's protection from evil, but we must also ask God to guard our thoughts and actions. We must begin to utilize His protection by filling our minds with positive thoughts and attitudes.

Are you prepared? How much sacrifice are you willing to make to see yourself moving to another level?

_____

_____

_____

_____

_____

Day 17

Motivation For The Harvest

"But thanks be to God! He gives us the victory through our Lord Jesus Christ. Therefore, my dear brothers and sisters, stand firm. Let nothing move you. Always give yourselves fully to the work of the Lord, because you know that your labor in the Lord is not in vain." (1 Corinthians 15:57-58 – NIV).

"Don't you have a saying, 'It's still four months until harvest'? I tell you, open your eyes and look at the fields! They are ripe for harvest." (John 4:35 - NIV).

What gives you the drive and passion? Open your eyes. Stop looking down; just look up and see what God has for you. There is a long process to get to any work harvest. Harvest is the result of labor—months of farming. You may have to rely on the rain combined with God's help. Can God trust you with more? Can He trust you with His most prized possession? The level of God trusting you will determine the harvest given to you.

Do you remember the parable of the three men and the talents that were given to them? (see Matthew 25:14-30). Are you willing to work hard for the harvest? Are you willing to manage the harvest? How is your relationship being single and looking to find a spouse? How are your finances, resources, and emotions? Learn to manage what you already have. If you mismanage little things, you will mismanage big things, then how will you get true riches?

Harvest is God's best for you. His trust grows when you trust His plans for your life. Praise God while reaping your harvest.

"I will bless the Lord at all times: his praise shall continually be in my mouth." (Psalm 34:1 – KJV).

Take a good, long look at your daily routine. How can you manage the harvest that God has given you? How can you add value to each aspect of your life?

"Repent ye therefore, and be converted, that your sins may be blotted out, when the times of refreshing shall come from the presence of the Lord." (Acts 3:19 – KJV).

"Those that be planted in the house of the Lord shall flourish in the courts of our God." (Psalm 92:13 – KJV).

"The righteous will flourish like a palm tree, they will grow like a cedar of Lebanon;" (Psalm 92:12 – NIV).

Day 18

God Is With You Even In Your Winter Season

Winter can illustrate a season of spiritual adversity. Song of Solomon 2:11-12 says "See! the winter is past; the rains are over and gone flowers appear on the earth, the season of singing has come, the cooing of doves is heard in our land. (NIV).

Never let problems, conflicts, or the difficulties in life ruin your ability to enjoy God's gifts. Take time to enjoy the world God created. Winter brings ice and an abundance of snow. Winter is the coldest season of the air between autumn and spring. Some winters in your lives can be your husband leaving you for another woman; you got fired from your job; financial difficulties. Some people go through depression during the winter.

In 2021, my family made the transition by moving to another state. The winter season was no comparison to what we were used to in New York. However, I had a winter situation. I had shingles, which is a reactivation of the chickenpox virus in the body, causing a painful rash with blisters. Never in my life have I felt so much pain and discomfort. The pain persisted even after the rash was gone. I would never want anyone to go through what I went through. My friend came to see me, and she was terrified. She called the pharmacy right there and then, and they said she could come and get vaccinated. Everyone that I told went and got vaccinated.

Winter in your life can be some painful experiences, like death, depression, grief, homelessness, aches and pains and the loss of strength and ability. However, your spring is coming, which will bring great messages of rebirth and hope in Christ Jesus. If you are not in your winter yet, it might come faster than you expect. Life goes by quickly.

Live today as if it is your last day. Smile. Say the things you want to say now. Life is a gift. Enjoy your moments with those you love. You have no promise that you will see all the seasons of your life. Ecclesiastes 3:1 says, "There is a time for everything, and a season for every activity under Heaven." (NIV). Spring is coming.

Many of us long for sunshine and spring. Genesis 8:22 says, "As long as the earth endures, seedtime and harvest, cold and heat, summer and winter, day and night will never cease." (NIV). God has a plan for all of us. God has promised never again to destroy everything on earth until judgment day when Christ returns. Now every change of season is a reminder of His promise. He provides cycles of life, each with its work for us to do. Although we may face many problems that seem to contradict God's plan, these should not be barriers to believing in Him but rather opportunities to discover that without God, life's problems have no lasting solutions!

I urge you to immerse yourself in Christ and the Word of God in order to preserve and renew yourself. It is a time of intimacy with God. The song says, "Draw me nearer, nearer, nearer blessed Lord to Thee." James 4:8a says, "Come near to God and He will come near to you." (NIV). Although we do not deserve God's favor, He reaches out to us in love and gives us worth and dignity, despite our human shortcomings.

Day 19

Encouragement For Today

Can you get away from discouragement to encouragement? The Bible tells us, "David encouraged himself in the Lord his God." (1 Samuel 30:6 - KJV). Likewise, you and I can find comfort in knowing we are not alone in our day-to-day issues. David encouraged himself by reflecting on the many times God delivered him from challenges. His confidence grew through his experiences.

How do you get through your tough times? It comes by strengthening yourself daily, knowing your Father God who is bigger than all your problems. I was strengthened by the many prayers that went up for me during my time. David was in a crisis. He returned home with his fighting men to discover that his town had been attacked while he was away. It was burned, and all the women and children had been taken, including David's two wives. There was a lot of crying and weeping. Anger flowed toward David. They planned to stone him to death. Faced with the tragedy of losing their families, David's soldiers began to turn against him and even thought about killing him. Instead of planning a rescue, they looked for someone to blame, but David found his strength in God and began looking for a solution instead of a scapegoat.

When facing problems, remember that it is useless to look for someone to blame or criticize. Instead, consider how you can help find a solution. David's relationship with God taught him complete dependency upon his God. "Even though I walk through the darkest valley, I will fear no evil, for you are with me; your rod and your staff, they comfort me." (Psalm 23:4 - NIV). Having a prayer life with God, fasting, and reading the Word of God will strengthen our souls for the times when it seems we are going to hit rock bottom.

How do we strengthen ourselves in the Lord? By building a relationship with Him. Remember the many things He has done for you in the past. You can keep a journal too. For me, I have verses all over my room, and I daily write what He has done for me. They are physical reminders to help me to be strong.

The ability to get through the toughest of times comes from strengthening yourself daily. Have you ever said, "I can't think of anything God has done for me. How can I praise Him?" We can praise Him for His great love towards us and His faithfulness that endures forever. If He did nothing else for us, He would still be worthy of our highest praise. (Hallelujah). Keep pursuing, keep pushing, keep fighting, you will recover it all. Be encouraged; it is not over until God says so.

What's your favorite Bible verse that you use to strengthen yourself?

_____

_____

_____

Day 20

Slow To Anger

"**M**y dear brothers and sisters, take note of this: Everyone should be quick to listen, slow to speak and slow to become angry, because human anger does not produce the righteousness that God desires." (James 1:19-20 – NIV).

The best way to develop this slowness to anger is to reflect frequently on the patience of God towards us. These verses speak of anger that erupts when our egos are bruised—"I am hurt" or "My opinions are not being heard." When sin and injustice occur, we should become angry because others are being hurt. We should not become angry when we fail to win an argument or when we feel offended or neglected.

Selfish anger helps no one. The parable of the unforgiving servant in Matthew 18:21-35 was designed to help us recognize our own need for patience towards others by recognizing the patience of God towards us. We are the unmerciful servant when we lose our patience under provocation. In essence, we ignore God's extreme patience with us.

Many times we discipline our children out of anger, while God disciplines us out of love. We are so eager to punish the person who provokes us, while God is eager to forgive us. We are eager to exercise our authority while God extends His love.

Why do you and I react out of anger and frustration? How can we stop? We need help! Yes, there is help.

"The Lord is gracious and compassionate, slow to anger and rich in love." (Psalm 145:8 - NIV).

Name some things that get you angry easily, and plan how you are going to work on your anger management.

_____

_____

_____

_____

_____

_____

_____

_____

_____

_____

_____

Day 21

Endorse Enlargement

Jabez was more honorable than his brothers. His mother had named him Jabez,[a] saying, "I gave birth to him in pain." Jabez cried out to the God of Israel, "Oh, that you would bless me and enlarge my territory! Let your hand be with me, and keep me from harm so that I will be free from pain." And God granted his request. (1 Chronicles 4:9-10 – NIV).

Jabez is remembered for a prayer request rather than a heroic act. In his prayer, he asked God to:

- Bless him.
- Enlarge his territory.
- Be with him in all he did.
- Keep him from evil and harm.

Jabez acknowledged God as the true center of his work. When we pray, we should ask God to take His rightful position in our lives. Jabez prayed specifically to be protected from harm and pain. We live in a fallen world filled with sin, and it is important to ask God to keep us safe from the unavoidable evil that comes our way. Can you see the predicament from his birth? Can you believe a mom would give her son a name that means pain? She bore him in sorrow; she had a difficult labor.

Today, be careful of the names you give to your children or names people call you. Guess what, God granted Jabez his request. God kept him from harm and freed him from all pain.

What is it that you want God to enlarge for you?

Take a few minutes and reflect on your life. Write down some ways you need enlargement in your life.

_____

_____

_____

_____

_____

_____

_____

_____

_____

_____

_____

_____

_____

_____

_____

Day 22

Is Your Gift Making Room For You?

"**A** man's gift maketh room for him, and bringeth him before great men." (Proverbs 18:16 - KJV).

One morning, at 4:05 am, I awoke and started praying. I did so for an hour. There, on my knees, God reminded me that I was an influencer and, according to His Word, my gift would make room for me. God put a gift in you, and by doing so, the world will make room for you. God enabled me to reach so many people.

Today, I do not look at what others do with their gifts. I am focusing on the gift that the Lord has given me. It is this gift that will enable me to fulfill my purpose. For a long time, things have been dormant inside me. I felt guilty that I was created for greatness. God had a plan for me, and I was doing nothing. I got up and decided I could offer something unique.

God is opening closed doors for me. It is not who you expect that will assist you. What do you have? Do you have an idea for a business? How long have you been thinking about that idea? Go for it: come up with a business plan. What kind of support system will you need? Get the right people interested in your idea. God created me to make a contribution. I am a carrier of His idea, so I could become a part of His creative team. You and I are a very important part of His plan.

There are seeds of greatness in all of us. It is time to make some power-move. Ask yourself, "What is in my hand?" Is it your gift or time?

Whatsoever thy hand findeth to do, do it with thy might; for there is no work, nor device, nor knowledge, nor wisdom, in the grave, whither thou goest. (Ecclesiastes 9:10 - KJV).

Myles Monroe said, "If you decide that you are going to find something that is truly yours then you will fulfill your vision, and you will be remembered by others."

Joseph had a gift of interpreting dreams that brought him before Pharoah. His other gift enabled him to store grain and get Egypt through a famine (see Genesis 40-41). Joseph's gifts were the key to his success.

David had a gift to play the harp that brought him before King Saul (see 1 Samuel 16:23). In exercising your gifts, you will find real fulfillment, purpose, and contentment in your life. You have everything within you to get the job done.

What could you begin to do now to develop the gift that is placed in you?

_____

_____

Day 23

Distractions—Do Not Let It Cause You To Lose Your Blessings

In Matthew 14:25-32, Jesus is walking on water, and He tells Peter to "Come." Peter saw the boisterous wind and became afraid, and he began to sink. A distraction is anything that prevents someone from giving full attention to something else, or an extreme agitation of the mind or emotions. When we are staring into the face of cancer, heart disease, high blood pressure, Covid, or some life-threatening illness, some of the first questions that come to mind are: Who is the doctor? What is his or her experience? Is he able to deal with my condition?

Distractions make us drift from our goals and keep us from living a productive life. With the help of God, you owe it to yourself to get rid of distractions, whether it be people, places, or things. Luke 10:38-42 tells the story of two sisters, Mary and Martha, who both loved Jesus. In verse 40, Martha was distracted by all the preparations that had to be made. Jesus said to Martha, "...you are worried and upset about many things, 42 but few things are needed—or indeed only one.[a]

Mary has chosen what is better, and it will not be taken away from her." (Luke 10:41b-42 - NIV). Jesus did not blame Martha for being concerned about household chores. He was asking her to set priorities.

Are you so busy doing things for Jesus that you are not spending time with Him? Do not let your service become self-serving. You cannot allow distractions to cause you to miss what God has for you. Myles Monroe said, "The greatest tragedy in life is not death, but a life without purpose." Personal attack hurts, and when the criticism is unjustified, it is easy to be distracted. When you are doing God's work, you will receive attacks on your character but pray and ask God to keep you focused.

"Thou wilt keep him in perfect peace, whose mind is stayed on thee: because he trusteth in thee." (Isaiah 26:3 – KJV). Distractions do not always have to be a problem or a situation that seems to be getting worse. Sometimes it can be a situation that seems all so right. For example, I know this guy who is not a Christian, but I am, and he really loves me. I am tempted to start a relationship with him. Another example is: I know this job is keeping me from church, but I am able to pay all my bills. These will cause you to miss out on the things God has for you and leave you asking yourself: Why didn't God help me? God was helping you, but you became distracted before it became manifested.

Review any insight from this chapter that are meaningful to you in learning how to stay focused and not be distracted.

_____

_____

Day 24

Jesus Is Our Source Of Life

" **I** am the vine, ye are the branches." (John 15:5a – KJV).

In today's society, technology is the norm. Everyone is connecting to the internet, but after gaining access and acquiring needed information, you disconnect until you are ready to use it again. Today, I want to tell you that the key to your potential, the key to a happy and productive life, is remaining attached to your source—being hooked up to Jesus Christ, the only true vine.

There are three phrases in John 15:5:

1. I am the True Vine.
2. You are the branches.
3. Abide in Me.

The word "vine" literally means "source of life." Have you ever seen a grapevine? It is a very interesting plant. The vine is the thick wooden part running from the ground up to the pole, and it is the only part of the plant that contains life. None of the life is in the branches; all of it is in the vine. Jesus said, "I am the true vine." God has to often prune the vines because He knows there is more life down in the roots.

God knows we are humans, and we fail many times. He has to clip some of the branches and cut off the old leaves that stop the vine from producing. If God did not clip the disobedience and the many other things in our lives, I do not know where many of us would be today. The result of abiding in the vine is that you and I will bear fruit, and our wish will be granted.

The relationship of the vine and its branches:

- Jesus abiding (see John 15:4). Jesus dwells in us because He is the true vine, we are the branches. A branch separated from its vine will not only fail to bear fruit on its own, but it will die.
- The Father abiding (see John 15:8).
- The believer abiding (see John 15:7).

Apart from Christ our efforts are useless.

The result of abiding in the vine is, you will:

- Bear fruit.
- Bear much more fruit.
- Get your wish granted.

Are you receiving the nourishment and life offered by Jesus Christ, the vine? If not, you are missing a special gift He has for you.

What could you begin to do now to develop a better relationship with God?

_____

_____

_____

_____

_____

_____

_____

_____

_____

_____

_____

_____

_____

_____

_____

_____

_____

_____

_____

_____

_____

Day 25

The Woman Of Destiny

Mary was a woman of destiny (see Luke 1:26-56). I am a woman of destiny. God also beckons us to be women of destiny. Luke 1:30 says, "And the angel said unto her, Fear not, Mary: for thou hast found favour with God." (NIV). Before we were formed in our mother's womb, God knew us, and He knew who we would become. Being a woman of destiny is determined by God Almighty.

The word "destiny" refers to the events that will happen to a particular person in the future. Where you come from doesn't matter. It matters how God determines the outcome and how He will set your life. God is the one who writes the script of your life.

The woman of destiny is surprised by the favor of God. Look at Mary! She was surprised by her place of prominence. Can you imagine her saying, "I, Mary, am going to give birth to the Son of God." Mary surrendered to the purpose and plan of God.

Whatever God is doing in your life, you must surrender to Him. God's favor doesn't automatically bring instant success or fame. His blessings on Mary, the honor of being the mother of the Messiah, would lead to much pain. Her peers would ridicule her; her fiancé would come close to leaving her; her son would be rejected and murdered. But through her son would come the world's only hope, and this is why Mary is praised by countless generations as the young girl who "found favor" with God. I can only imagine some of the names people started to call her and the labels they put on her. Little did they know that Mary was a woman of destiny.

It can be painful when God interrupts your plans. Imagine Mary being pregnant, and it was not for Joseph. Today, as you read, don't wait to see the bottomline before offering your life to God. Offer your life willingly even when the outcome seems disastrous. As God's children, we must take responsibility for what God has deposited in us.

Do you know who you are? I am a woman of destiny. When you know God has deposited something in your life, you will keep the right company. Look at who Mary sought out; her cousin, Elizabeth—someone who had a similar experience because she was pregnant too.

The woman of destiny is a worshipper. Mary said, "My soul doth magnify the Lord." (Luke 1:46 - KJV). The woman of destiny will worship, work and war.

"Righteousness will be his belt and faithfulness the sash around his waist." (Isaiah 11:5 – NIV).

As a woman of destiny, stay focused. Do not abort your dreams. If God said so, it is so no matter how long the wait.

Take a few minutes and reflect on your life. Write down the ways you were encouraged to excel in your life. Were these ways more helpful or a hindrance to your understanding of your destiny?

_____

_____

_____

_____

_____

_____

_____

_____

_____

_____

_____

_____

_____

_____

_____

_____

_____

_____

Day 26

The Value Of Our Time

66"To every thing there is a season, and a time to every purpose under the heaven:" (Ecclesiastes 3:1 - KJV).

We should make the best of our time because the days are evil. In today's society, there are so many books and seminars to tell us how to manage our time. I believe it is not so much more information we need but more discipline. So, you may ask: What is the purpose of making the most of our time? Realizing that time is short helps us use the little time we have more wisely. The Bible says, "Teach us to number our days, that we may gain a heart of wisdom." (Psalm 90:12 - NIV). Because our days are numbered, we want our work to count, to be effective and productive. We desire to see God's eternal plan revealed in our lives.

We should use our time effectively. Many of us waste our time over the years doing dumb things and making poor decisions. I was a fool to do some things, but now I have become wise. I put closure on them, and my time is spent better than yesterday. How effective you live is what is important.

Many of us have messed up, but it is not too late. There are friends you need to drop and people you need to associate yourself with who will help you get to your destiny. Proverbs 18:24 says, "One who has unreliable friends soon comes to ruin, but there is a friend who sticks closer than a brother." (NIV). We all need friends who will stick close, listen, care and offer help when it is needed—in good times and bad. It is better to have one such friend than dozens of superficial acquaintances. Instead of wishing you could find a true friend, seek to become one. There are people who need your friendship. Ask God to reveal them to you, and then take on the challenge of being a true friend.

The song says, "One day at a time, sweet Jesus, that is all I'm asking from You." The more time we spend with God praying and meditating on His Word, the more we find our focus in life changing from self-centeredness to Christ-centeredness.

I responded to God's love for me early in my life. I know that God's love for me is unconditional. Because of my security and worth in Jesus Christ, I do not have to look to people or things to feel of value or loved. I trust my needs to be met by my heavenly Father, including the value of my time.

What small steps could you take towards the purpose of your time?

_____

_____

_____

Day 27

How Persistent Are You In Prayer?

In Luke 11:5-13, Jesus taught a parable about a man whose friend arrived at midnight, but he had nothing to serve him. He banged on the friend's door waking him up, and asked to borrow some bread. Can you imagine someone coming to you at 2 am asking to borrow money or bread from you? The man insisted that he could not get up, but Jesus said: "I tell you, even though he will not get up and give you the bread because of friendship, yet because of your shameless audacity he will surely get up and give you as much as you need. "So I say to you: Ask and it will be given to you; seek and you will find; knock and the door will be opened to you." (NIV).

What does it mean to be persistent? It is the quality that allows someone to continue doing something or trying to do something, even though it seems difficult or opposed by other people. Persistence or boldness in prayer overcomes our insecurities. Practicing persistence does more to change our hearts and minds more than God, and it helps us understand and express the intensity of our need.

Persistence in prayer helps us to recognize God's work. So often, it seems that God waits till the last possible moment to answer desperate prayers. Just as often, a critical deadline passes without an answer, and you ask, "Where is God?" At times we do not know what to pray for, but the Holy Spirit intercedes on our behalf. Roman 8:26 says, "In the same way, the Spirit helps us in our weakness. We do not know what we ought to pray for, but the Spirit himself intercedes for us through wordless groans." (NIV). Sometimes we push away people we should keep and keep people we should push away. We sometimes have a degree of ignorance, many times, because of fear and doubt that paralyzes us from achieving our goals. We are not left to our own resources to cope with problems. Even when you do not know the right words to pray, the Holy Spirit prays with and for you, and God answers. Do not be afraid. Bring your requests to God, trust that He will always do what is best for you according to His will for your life.

As you move forward, keep a positive mental attitude. Make it your determination that you will endeavor to learn new skills and not allow others to tell you who you are. Get up from your comfort zone and grab what is out there for you.

I came to America as an international student and, of course, the journey was very hard at times, but I was very persistent, and today I am who God wants me to be. Many of us go through life praying a little, planning a little, hoping, but never being quite certain of anything, and always secretly afraid that we will miss the way. This is a waste of truth. We were created for greatness. Be persistent, there is a light at the end of the tunnel.

Your social status does not limit God when He has a plan for you. He will reach into the background and bring you into the foreground. Be persistent in all your endeavors.

Name some things that hinder you from being persistent:

_____

_____

_____

_____

_____

_____

_____

_____

Day 28

How Are You Managing What Is Entrusted In Your Hands?

In Luke 16:1-12, Jesus told an unusual story about management. It is about a smart manager who happened to be dishonest but who really had the makeup of an excellent manager. Jesus commended him for what he did after he was fired. He was fired for wasting his master's property and for lying about it. He was stunned when his master told him to leave. Finding another job was hard for him so he went and found his master's debtors. He sat down with each of them and renegotiated the amount of money that was outstanding on their bills. Jesus made a very important point, "Whoever can be trusted with very little can also be trusted with much, and whoever is dishonest with very little will also be dishonest with much." (Luke 16:10 - NIV). If you mismanage little things, you will mismanage big things, then how will you get true riches? Our integrity often meets its match in money matters.

God called us to be honest, even in small details. We could easily rationalize away heaven's riches, which are far more valuable than earthly wealth. Money has the power to take

God's place in your life; it can become your master. How can you tell if you are a slave to money?

1. Do you think and worry about it frequently?
2. Do you give up doing what you should do or would like to do in order to make more money?
3. Do you spend a great deal of your time caring for your possessions?
4. Is it hard to give money away?
5. Are you in debt?

Let us use our resources wisely because they belong to God and not to us. Joseph was a foreigner and prisoner. Yet, he was promoted by his management skills by Pharaoh. Pharaoh put him in charge of the whole country. As an employee, do you just show up to collect your paycheck? As a receptionist at a front desk, are you alert, friendly, and reliable? As the janitor behind the scenes, do you work effectively? Regardless of your position, you can come up with ideas to make your employer's business grow.

Money can be used for good and evil. Money has a lot of power; we must use it carefully and thoughtfully. We live in an age that measures people's worth by how much money they make. We can have peace of mind and security if we listen to what God is saying about money, or do we laugh about what He is saying about serving money? We are to make wise use of the financial opportunities we have. Take a good long look at your daily routine. How can you manage it better? How can you add value to each aspect of it?

Is there any area you think you could have done better with what God has entrusted in your hands?

_____

_____

_____

_____

_____

_____

_____

_____

_____

_____

_____

_____

_____

_____

_____

_____

_____

_____

_____

Day 29

Do Not Give Up

In Genesis 29:16-30, the story is told of Jacob working hard for seven years to marry the love of his life, Rachel, who was the younger of two sisters. The father, Laban, deceived Jacob and gave the older daughter, Leah, in marriage to Jacob. It was the custom of the land that the older child married first. Jacob had to work another seven years of hard labour to get Rachel. People often wonder if working a long time for something they desire is worth it. I believe it does. The most important goals and desires are worth working and waiting for. Patience is the hardest when we need it the most, but it is the key to achieving our goals.

There is this song that says, "I just can't give up now. I've come too far from where I have started from. Nobody told me that the road would easy, and I don't believe He brought me this far to leave me."

There are many victories, breakthroughs, successes, and achievements that only come after long seasons of what seem like fruitless efforts. The sad reality is, many of these victories never come simply because people give up and quit too soon.

There are days, weeks, and years of working and waiting with little to show. It can take a toll on your heart and spirit. Let us be honest; it is hard to keep going when everything inside is screaming "quit." Many people leave and lose when victory was right around the corner. When you are faced with the choice between continuing to fight a hopeless battle or allowing yourself the relief of giving up, how do you choose?

Jacob never gave up even though the odds were against him. In Genesis 29, Jacob did everything, both right and wrong, with great zeal. He deceived his own brother, Esau, and his father, Isaac. He wrestled with an angel and worked for fourteen years to marry the woman he loved. Was Jacob treated unfairly? Yes, without question. So many of us go through life saying, "It is not fair." True, but God never promised that the world would treat us fairly. If God allowed His only Son to die for us while He was innocent of any wrongdoing, do you think He will exempt us from unjust treatment? No way.

For the most part, godly character is not developed in the good times of life but in the bad. Godly character is developed in your life as you respond positively to unjust treatment. Isn't that what Romans 5:3-4 tells us? "Not only so, but we also glory in our sufferings, because we know that suffering produces perseverance; perseverance, character; and character, hope." (NIV). Whatever it is that God wants to do in your life, let Him do it. Do not give up.

Life is hard, overwhelming, and painful, but please do not give up. Things may be at its worst, but God is with you. Strengthen the things that are about to die in your life. Many people give up just short of achieving their goals and dreams. If they had endured a little longer, then victory and triumph would be theirs. Your dreams might be getting through school but studying is so hard. Continue to work hard to achieve all that God has planned for you. There will be difficulties and discouragement on the road to your success. Winners never quit, and quitters never win. God's power is not limited by a lack of fair play. He has the ability to meet our needs and make us thrive, even though others mistreat us. To give in and respond is to be no different from your enemies.

What are some stumbling blocks you are facing in your goal to stay focused and not give up?

_____

_____

_____

_____

_____

_____

_____

_____

_____

_____

_____

_____

_____

_____

Day 30

Fear Not, God Hears Your Prayers

But the angel said to him: "Do not be afraid, Zechariah; your prayer has been heard. Your wife Elizabeth will bear you a son, and you are to call him John." (Luke 1:13 – NIV).

How would you feel if you were to hear those words in your ears about a situation you have been waiting for an answer to? It could be mixed reactions; maybe. Zacharias was not experiencing a dream or vision—the angel appeared in a visible form and spoke audible words to him. Here was this couple who shared the pain of not having children, and they had passed the age of childbearing too. If we want our prayers answered, we must be open to what God can do in impossible situations. We must wait for God to work in His way and in His time.

You may have been waiting for years on God; maybe waiting for your immigration documents, finding the right person to marry, buying a new home, etc. Maybe your marriage is a mess, and you need an answer. You may be searching for a job, or you have a lovely home, kids are doing great, but your health is a great issue. The thing you desire the most may not be given to you yet, but God delivers on time. You can have complete confidence that God will keep His promises.

Fear is a natural reaction to news that makes you lose your joy. God has not given you a spirit of fear but of power, and of love and of a sound mind. (see 2 Timothy 1:7). Stop being afraid! Your prayer has been heard. God has a way of saying things to you that make no sense. When you think of prayer, it is a conversation with God; you talk to Him and tell Him how you feel. He knows your thoughts, but He loves when you converse with Him.

"Pray without ceasing." (1 Thessalonians 5:17 - KJV).

God hears you when you pray; it does not go on deaf ears.

"And this is the confidence that we have in him, that, if we ask any thing according to his will, he heareth us:"(1 John 5:14 – KJV).

God does not only hear but He answers. Your answer is on its way. Do not stop praying for what you need—continue praying; you are almost there. He may not come when you want Him, but He will be there right on time. It might not be the next day, but it will be the proper time.

If you are waiting for God to answer some request or to fill some need, remain patient. No matter how impossible it may seem, what He said in His Word will come through at the right time. For me, I came to America and, at one point, I lived in a rented house for more than eighteen years. I worked, I prayed,

I fasted, I cried, I waited. I trusted in God, and today He has not only heard my prayer, but He has answered my prayer and blessed me with a beautiful home.

Name some things you have been praying to God about. How do you feel at this point? Do you think He is taking too long to answer?

_____

_____

_____

_____

_____

_____

_____

_____

_____

_____

_____

_____

_____

_____

_____

_____

About the Author

Anita McInnis is a licensed pastoral counselor. She holds a master's degree in Christian counseling from the National Christian Counselors Association (NCCA). She is also a licensed marriage officer. She has an associate degree in Hotel and Restaurant Management from Hocking College, Nelsonville, Ohio, and a Bachelor in Business Management from Monroe College, New Rochelle, New York.

Anita is married to the love of her life, Alvin, for over thirty years, and she is the proud mother of two sons, Sean and Stephen.

Made in the USA
Columbia, SC
02 August 2023

21088434R00050